THE DECLINE AND FALL
OF THE CHATTY EMPIRE

THE HUGH MacLENNAN POETRY SERIES

Editors: Allan Hepburn and Carolyn Smart

Recent titles in the series

The Decline and Fall
of the Chatty Empire

JOHN EMIL VINCENT

McGill-Queen's University Press

Montreal & Kingston • London • Chicago

ISBN 978-0-2280-1704-2 (paper)
ISBN 978-0-2280-1738-7 (ePDF)
ISBN 978-0-2280-1739-4 (ePUB)

Legal deposit second quarter 2023
Bibliothèque nationale du Québec

Printed in Canada on acid-free paper that is 100% ancient forest free
(100% post-consumer recycled), processed chlorine free

We acknowledge the support of the Canada Council for the Arts.

Nous remercions le Conseil des arts du Canada de son soutien.

Library and Archives Canada Cataloguing in Publication

Title: The decline and fall of the chatty empire / John Emil Vincent.

Names: Vincent, John Emil, 1969- author.

Series: Hugh MacLennan poetry series.

Description: Series statement: The Hugh MacLennan poetry series

Identifiers: Canadiana (print) 20220452571 | Canadiana
(ebook) 20220452598 | ISBN 9780228017042 (softcover) |
ISBN 9780228017387 (ePDF) | ISBN 9780228017394 (ePUB)

Classification: LCC PS3622.I532 D43 2023 | DDC 811/.6—dc23

This book was typeset by Marquis Interscript in 9.5/13 Sabon.

THE DECLINE AND FALL
OF THE CHATTY EMPIRE: *an epyllion*

for Virginia Konchan
and
for Jason Camlot

CONTENTS

Bread and Circus

"*Be careful, Pinocchio! These bad friends of yours will end up by making you lose your love for our books. I hope they won't lead you into any great trouble.*"

"*Oh, there's no such danger!*" answered the puppet, shrugging his shoulders, and touching his forehead with his finger as if to say, "*There's too much good sense up here inside!*"

Carlo Collodi

Epyllion

I know you're hurting.
What loser's not really
just a beaten winner?

Here, this is my impression of you all being glum . . .
Cathy had gone too far
and the girls knew

when to pack it in.
And so they did.
Window gratings eyed them

warily but a little achingly.
They crunched over crack vials
to the place they knew

flowers bloomed and beauty
was an inevitability: the dump.
Some funny guy

in full mime do
was stuck in a box
no matter how fast

he climbed that rope.
And in the wind too!
But the box dimensions grew

and grew. A nightmare!
Cathy shat herself awake.
Oh, ooooooo. She got mad.

I will never Mister Professor sir
mark my words, ever
watch Italian films

before bed. No one was
awake to hear her. In fact
she was alone in a long row

of cots in a barracks
miles underground
surrounded by the vague

fish-in-a-barrel fireworks of war above.
She screamed her string short.
Know how you feel –

the face of Sigourney Weaver
hovered huge before Cathy.
O Sigourney, angel of artillery,

just buff enough still to save me …
No, I'm from that slide projector
right over there. I don't know

why any of us ever
trusts the other. Well I don't know
any continental philosophy whatever, Cathy replied.

For now, though, I'm sad
I'm alonely
and fain would go home.

I want my Mamma.
Cathy's Mamma
was a long retired

outdated, much insulted machine.
An early prototype of what poets
and pundits alike would one day use shamelessly

to stand for hope.

Of course there was paperwork.
For that they had Mr Professor. Despite
being short a degree and an annoying propensity

to make everything "a teaching moment,"
his tallies always totaled out.
This contract, he sniffed,

is toilet paper.
C'mon, Cathy coaxed, just vet it.
No, I mean it's toilet paper.

They hit the other agencies.
On foot. Only some stops
for glue application

and huffing. Trudgingly,
near blue, they reached The Riddler's Lair
in whose ashtray

Barb stubbed her Virginia
Slim so hard it buckled.
The Riddler, turns out,

retired, leaving only
his leotard of question marks on a dummy.
Fitting, quipped Cathy,

who snagged her string on a coat hook
to muster vim and inspire vigor
in the fading starlets.

Two corn cob handles
square off
only to collapse

back into their own
with fantasies, each one, of darting foils,
daring feints, clanks and jabs.

No duel? demanded Chatty Cathy,
but of course the inanimate
speak only themselves:

In this case seamed plastic cobs,
garish yellow, wielding sharpened
tuning forks.

Well, pull my string,
they've made up, or resigned themselves
to a life of identical woe.

Alas, all crisis comes
with its own kit and sometimes
skill sets got at the Y.

CPR, for instance, Cathy mused.
Her mind, unlike the others,
was syruped like pears.

Theirs were lumpy futons
that didn't start very comfortable. Please,
she clapped, some cheer.

Fer fuck's sake, Cathy.
Georgia had lost her teeth
and faith. God bankrupted her.

What God, she steamed,
would dictate dildoes and boobie keychains
over bibles in a Christian bookstore –

And also God, while we got you,
why do good things happen
to bad people? Her teeth

were strung round the neck
of DeeDee of the badass girlgang
called First National. A trophy.

Georgia still seethed when
she'd see DeeDee on the front page
handing some misfit toys

a gigantic cardboard check.
The teeth there – round her neck.
Bygones, Cathy chirped,

Buck up.
To hell with
frowns and good advice, girls,

we're goin' syndicated!
It was so long since joy had knocked
its brass hand-shaped handle on their

variously complex voice boxes
that the cheer that went up
scared starlings from yon hedge,

lovers from ere sedge. It was
the last chortle Georgia
would ever chuck,

the final teehee, yuck, snort,
heh heh, hee hee, poo on you,
she'd shout.

Rumor is: the roofies worked
too well. She wandered
St Louis whistling.

Of course you know
Cathy can't whistle!
Just as some reputations

founder for years in shallows
or are snagged eagerly
and tied to a ramshackle dock

then neglected, so did
the Girls continue their decade.
As if through binoculars

passed one to the other
like a flask.
Other lives

clambered over them,
sat on their heads.
Cathy recovered her diamonds.

They were fake, sure,
but may's well have been
each tear she'd shed

in pursuit of whatever
it was that motivated her
to always find exactly the wrong

fella. Mutual dysfunction
was her analyst's take,
her dentist felt differently.

Then again she married *him*.
Only dated the shrink. Days poured
over a cement wall called

picturesquely a "dam,"
though the creek could
only be spared ridicule

if you called it a "crick."
Ah, but aren't all utterances
shards of one great utterance

or rather are all utterances
collected in one particular
atmospheric layer

where they slide over each other
sexy as snakes in a coffin.
And us: blasé snake handlers.

Cathy! Cathy! Gypsy May slapped her.
Come back, come back to us.
O. Why on earth'd she slip herself more roofie?

Rehab was abbreviated.
The macramé owls Cathy
knotted convinced Matron

of her total hopeless desire
to preserve what must inevitably
fall to the timber industry.

Incurable. But this one, a perfect
Snorting Striped Antlered Owl
native to one tree in Northern Washington State

and that tree actually
a cell phone tower.
A rare breed indeed.

They were shelved. But
doesn't that in the end
mean preserved? Held for

an appropriate time rather than
cast like seed on rocky ground.
Cathy gave up hoping

which more than suited the others
whose joints required tools
long lost in toy boxes

long lost. Arthritic
they moved less
but became kinder

and maybe wiser
what with the waiter
using a dedicated scraper

to elegantly decrumb
the fresh cleared linen.
Now they could see

what had eluded them.
There had been an event
to which they had gone

at an appointed hour
and sat behind their name tent
and puzzled over an embarrassment of forks

and ate without knowing it snail
and listened to their life story
told in broad strokes

in watercolor.
Raised their glass
to having things in common

listened to anecdotes
lifted from National Public Radio
and claimed their cars from valets.

The quiet ride home,
the lights on in each cavernous room
only to walk through,

the talk of how flowers bring life
to life, and the puffy pillows,
satin as an old woman's face

who has had several acid peels
and isn't giving up,
and then sinking

back into themselves.
This is what life is about:
One thousand thread count sheets.

Amazing how real life is
lived only by the wealthy.
But each sighs in her sleep:

if there is life to live
best to live it in tribute
to those left behind

though all our words
end up the same place
atangle. Priced

by the pound.
So why waste them?
Cathy was back to her insipid self:

Let's play some charades!

Rarely when the senator
you've been waiting for
to die does

do you celebrate.
If it's bad taste
no matter,

Gypsy May nearly shouted,
popping a cork
into a napkin.

Around, the roar
she recalled from zombie films
where the hero's

eyes roll down
for just long enough
to get

a bead
on the shit he's in
but also

bring down
from his inner head
the scent of brain.

Capers and pileups
of the undead on the nation's highways
result. May sometimes

runs her fingers over the ridge
around good taste, pushing along
a growing wedge of fuzzy dust,

the point: to launch
her into dreams
where doilies can't

claim territory
or bully
the just regular flatware

with intricacy.
May longs for flesh,
teeth-torn and handheld

in flickers and creaking cranks
of spits not yet far along
enough to lubricate themselves.

The good days that now
seem like a very well made up
corpse. Then, she had a yeast

infection nonstop.
But recalls only the back
of a hand running

cheek to earlobe,
the crunch of bedding
and the wild stares

of winter. She casts
handfuls of pills
over her shoulder

and, sure, they
just clatter on the tiles
behind

but kids do recover,
so alarmingly often in fact, that two
or three suspicious types worry.

But no one listens to them
anyhow; they eat skunk,
and beside that stink.

The worriers. Too bad
they never inherit anything
but their share.

One back there, in the past,
worth a drift off to a copse of ganglia with:
Sharon, who began each sentence:

"My generals." Sharon crushed
May's face to her body.
Fists full of her hair

as if threatening to yank
it all out
if the fingers weren't soon

forced open by ecstasy.

VIII

Seeing as the Pledge
specifically bans knife fights,
Mindy had some explaining.

Her defense was defense.
But also, she claimed, a shiv
is not a knife.

The council concurred on this.
Shivs, though, do come under
the arts and crafts skill provision

whereby special skills
excepting extraordinary skills,
for instance, Barb's crank-in-able hair,

or Julie's see-through skin, –
such skills as can, must be taught the entire clan.

Or else they signal
pathological craftiness
and resistance to co-optation

into a truly
modern aesthetic.
So, there was a workshop.

There were cupcakes,
sinks of ricin and anthrax,
and a meth lab

built of Lincoln logs and
twisty straws. Everyone smiled.
Mindy not least of all.

IX

As Samantha rolled the last
of the foil over the final window
to forever banish the punishing

diuretic of time
and lock in freshness
– a last resort –

her nail sped the edges
and folded down the corners
neat as a military action.

When the phone rang.
It was for real. It was too much.
It was just great.

Sign Us Up, said Cathy.
She missed the cradle
with the receiver,

looked annoyed,
hung the phone up with too much care
and then up came:

That new network
wants has-beens.
Wannabes have had it.

But, May interrupted,
doesn't that make the wannabes ...
Cathy flathanded,

then curled
her huge long orange
nails to a fist.

Our letter, O Mary Ellen you GEEEnius,
was the thing he said.
The tone of humility

so naked and the despair
while not obvious in the nouns
screaming from the verbs

caught his eye. We are each to have:
A dressing room! A cheer went up.
Another flat Cathyhand. Then silence, then fist.

And makeovers! A roar. O to have been
an anthropologist on the wall
just then!

X

Powermad? Tell the bitch
I have ten minutes
a pipe full of rock

and no intention of
her lardass slowing me down.
No, tell her, be polite:

"Thanks honey, great work.
You're just not what Ms Chatty needs now.
She wants something, well, something not FIRED!"

Collapsing into Drucilla Deville postures
was now *de rigueur* for the greatest
has-been the viewing public

ever felt so much better than.
Unlike Drucilla, Cathy really
didn't have specific desires

which left her stealing
those of others, further
rocketing her awkward

and shamed figure
up the magazine rack
and there in garish four-colour glare

her
bearing alien twins,
smoking a Cuban cigar.

Sherry fell to drink.
May to indecisiveness or permissiveness.
Georgia back to religion.

The rest toadied,
making them unstoppably
more abject daily.

Insane demands issued.
Chatty Cathy would smirk.
Then by some horrible miracle

the girls would muster gusto
or ingenuity enough
to give one a foot up

over the ivied brick wall
of human dignity
into that most secret garden

of power. How high
the ratings read. Cathy
nibbling dolphin fin

and carrying on on camera
about some cook show host
and how, by tomorrow, .

he would be the buffet.

Police combed the area.
Abandoned buildings were gassed.
All in hopes of rescuing

Cathy from breach of contract.
Stupid as she was, Cathy wasn't stupid.
Her expiration date showed.

She tore fast as those heels
could teeter toward skid row
and her own true desuetude.

May decided to can the has-been circuit.
Sam too.
They pled guilty.

And now tend sheep
in documentaries in Nova Scotia.
Mary Ellen sells seashells somewhere.

And Sherry dried out long enough
to expire miserable. Though not miserably
as feared. Triumph isn't just

living through life. There's an ingredient,
extra, not in the recipe, Cathy knew that.
It's a matter of how long long is

and if it can be pinched closed
and cauterized. Cathy, amid trash,
lay back on her string's ring

uncomfortable as it was.
Couldn't she have been born
anorectic or to pee when pressed?

Why'd *her* name
have to so perfectly
fit the marquee?

SPQCathy

i.

What you love
will be taken from you;
eras and music you like

that once spilled
onto the esplanade
trimmed with chatter

and happiness –
they will pass.
The stones that now

so neatly if tackily
frame walks
will skew.

One day God will drop his cigar
in his coffee
and leave without tipping.

Your favourite versions
of yourself will flicker
then gutter

and killer amoebas
will attack and set
the theatre aflame.

And that's the reason
my Mom named me
Tootles.

The faces around
the picnic table
were biblical.

A new story
perhaps a parable
about a band of girls

sent into the fashion
magazine of their fantasy,
commissioned to find

the next trend in fur.
"*" Cathy slapped flat
every delicate angle

of a mosquito
and the spell
was broken.

Purple tacky clouds
replaced roseate
stained glass ones

and the tree line
walled itself up.
Well, Tootles,

with a mouthful of potato salad,
said:
thought you might fall for that one.

Their talents were heaped
and hued as a royally commissioned
still life of the fruit of the realm.

I'd have wondered what
exactly was
in the chest

they draped over:
one reciting nursery rhymes,
one enhancing self-images

with vague affirmations.
One in oven mitts.
When I first saw *Rope*

I found it romantic
and hated Jimmy Stewart
for firing out the window

rather than at the murderous boys
who ought then to have
swooned dying on the chest

heaped as deer on a hood
and given one another
a look unclouded

with consequence. Cathy
had the idea
of champagne flutes

for one and all
and in this photo
the famous photographer took

on his way between whoring
his talent to the diamond industry
and dining with a rent boy

who he'd give a modest
but designer ring,
so avant garde, however,

it couldn't be worn. Only admired, but
which fit their three-evening-long
romance. Conceptual

like this photo:
he focused on the reflection
on one flute where

the girls are by Van Eyck
favoured with the figures
and long foreheads

of the Dutch.

Barb's penchant for definition
left her prey to the regional.
She'd read the minor litrachers

for purities untackled
on floodlit fields;
unprotected conjectures

that seemed, though not tamed,
to come right up to her,
soft meaty mouth near-tickling

as it mopped the sugar cube
or apple or on occasion the muffin
from her palm. Twisted across the plain

her history included homicides
and concluded feuds, the frame
of the house she was born in

still stands against the palest
blue sky like it's waiting
to be filled with concrete.

Some days the games
of the jeering prairie dogs
weary her, others

the old roadkill
in a hostile takeover,
make her love life.

Such treasons
of the imagination –
that she could

be on one side
just as well as
on the other

but wherever she was
she was stuck there
until some new formula

wiped out the traditional ways,
or corralled them back,
stamping mad as they inevitably would be.

The cell lost its signal.
Greasy smoke slid beside
sketchy vineyards.

The smell was almost chemical.
But what, Barb corrected Midge,
isn't?

He was one stool
from a Nobel
when they married.

Whimsical, test tubes
were clinked
to their future.

They quickly discovered
a tech took
the wrong rack.

Large Marge
was already passed out:
her people

dead
and her friends
missing or in prison.

His were always right,
invented napalm,
and munched on egg salad.

She came downstairs late morning.
Someone gurgled from the sprawl.
She thought: some party.

As one ought stand warned
when someone says
I like you, I really do

so Ruby would have
been well-served
to hesitate between

the design and the construction
of her dream home.
The shape of a candy cane

in whose crook
a fountain spewed
water from the holes

in Billy the Kid's vest
and sleeve. Half-built
she paced past

what would be the trophy room
the beer hall
the museum

and she ransacked
her heritage for what
she might have overlooked.

Fuck all did she forget?
Ah! she thought,
they could always

empty the fountain and hang game
to bleed dry from Billy's arms
that reached only rib cage high

in attempted surrender.

Bread and Circus

a.

Injury the guide explained
is what
guides explain.

Sometimes a plaque,
others a bench.
Asterisks worn in brush.

In sand.
Built to boardwalks.
And if there is a star

it refers to
Sam was sure
a footnote.

And if there is a page,
a biographer, bookstores,
slick flack-jacket smile shots.

A web from which the injured
sends elegant signals,
the tenderest whiffs

of feeling.
But
jack-knifed

there
at the foot
of the stairs

she knew:
that the web
was not silk –

that the blood
sticky
pooled

'round her head –
was the lure
and had caught her.

b.

Ash in an urn
is more star
than after hours

the zoned headliner screaming her own name.
Tonight, understudied
by an up-and-comer

whose curls
smooth red as Nembutals
trembled with held notes – .

But the alley
generous as alleys are
when it's too late

to bother with creepy
from its diaphragm
delivers to windows

gone golden
the cry –
and each working Joe

each walk-up
bathroom-down-the-hallway
Jane

feels
not irritated
not worried about ·

tomorrow's wing nuts
tonight's heat –
rather, feels,

behind the fogged winter window:
like the finger
given something to write,

something the dawn
will hose down
unread by a soul:

the dripping
cursive so perfect.
But the lights

shrink to a TV dot
while the star grows
into her stupor.

Hundreds and hundreds
of messages
sent

to their senders
who
pulling up the sateen

ridge of a blanket
feel its cool
on their fingers

and with the other
useful fingers snap
the lamp off

and wonder what
could be worse
than your name

given you in spades.
To be
in sodium light

only
what you were once,
to feel

it fill you –
a hard gulp
a fist of booze

stretching its steely
muscled arms
in a yawn.

Most had outgrown
corner stores
for pharmacies.

So malt liquor out
Cathy insisted
on this

the fifth (giggles)
year mark of Sherry's death,
they drink five-year-old Scotch.

Too rich for picnics precisely,
they met at the same spot
with its willows

their schools of leaves
.razoring to and fro
with the wind,

the lake
and the clouds,
all catered.

Each cloche
softly rung open
ohs oos and ahs –

and the Scotch
in cut crystal.
Each felt

satisfaction no lowly thing
and tinkled then clinked
their glasses.

To Sherry.
And that nothing
ever satisfy.

To her vocational
doubts. To her
whose life

seemed a toy box of loss.
That we never ask:
why try.

Cathy toasted then
to the answers
of questions

to their dear
dead deluded friend.
To broken nails

and bruised ankles.
To Caring.
Jojo raised her glass

and added:
and to the need
for evidence

in the most obvious case
and the thrill finding
what was without question.

To all that that
may never have come forward
thinking it tacky.

May we be
powdered
in the sift.

Let history
Take
like chemicals

to special paper.
May we be
That Special Paper!

Clinks.
And the handpicked
young waiter

pale
hair so black
his stubble fell

like a shadow
across his bird-bone jaw.
And, Jojo added,

perhaps in tribute to him,
to all the agencies,
agents, form letters,

contracts, databases,
and grinding
daily need

that make mourning glamorous.

d.

Comeuppance all around,
the past pulled
its chips to its chest.

To admit timidity
was all
Cathy could muster.

There are other games,
she whispered,
better games. And ducked from the table.

There are days
Mars leaves a red chalk smear
on the ozone

and matchsticks
stand at attention.
They'd remove their

little white caps
could they,
handsome

as solemn jockeys
at a prize horse's
televised funeral.

Cathy knew such days.
She'd watch vinyl siding
sweat with it.

The luck of the draw
and the living with
good fortune exacted.

She'd heard tell
in tabloids
of luck being

mere patience,
being standoffishness
to the present.

She knew from luck.
But knowing,
disqualified.

e.

Then again
what is a picnic
but gloating.

That need can be met: arguable.
That Tupperware
fits it: dubious.

The reality
into which
you bite:

one of
exception. –

With the churning
clouds' whipped sugar
and the foam amid rocks

half-beaten egg white,
and the waterfall
all physics experiment

and the clearing
mowed by a failed
novelist.

Is it celebration
or the fragile
declaration

of détente
which hides
weapons

proliferating among themselves
so quickly
the counters barely

spin digits
fast enough
and never click

finished or hope
to find the combination
to open the safe.

Inside
ten women
a Jell-O mold

and a mandala
of deviled eggs
blessed

by the powder
a pinch a piece
of paprika.

f.

You know how you
want to see the character who says
"everything will be fine"

squashed.
Because they know
how they must be

both inevitably right
and also wrong
and that by the time

of either
no one will hold them
to it.

That was how Rita
rubbed you. Even
could she be trusted

with the future
she'd surely
with such a skill

feel superior.
As it was
she neither

knew
and even
having known

would
just like you
reading this

have forgotten
come the reckoning
what she'd said.

Only those
who suspect
backtracking likely

need
recall
all

they say.
Would that she
knew the outcome

for sure,
her knowing
wouldn't be

oily,
but piss
and vinegar

confidence,
for which, truth be told,
we'd hate her anyway.

g.

Only mid-tundra
did Cathy just know
she'd need a new agent.

Five a.m. and Chatty Cathy
chafed the day.
Her team

wouldn't you know it,
the nice not the driven
ones, licking her.

Yes, indeed, they did
look calendaresque
pulling her while she pulled

on a long white menthol cigarette
and now and then
she'd cry hyah!

The dogs had first chance
pissed a hole and dropped
her whip in it.

Later, the grocery store gossip rags
would host
o-mouthed Cathy

teetering
clutching a bottle.
But

you could clearly see,
she proudly plunked her
frozen dinner on the register,

that throughout, she hadn't
broken, hadn't lost and to the end
lurched on, her fire-engine red stilettos.

h.

How, having forgotten all the children
Huddled around your four-candled cake
In the faded, round-cornered photo,
Your eyes have eyes only for you,
So did Cathy scan the kiosk.

And finding herself, as if readying a bray,
Grinned. The wedding had FULL COVERAGE,
Her smearing the cake, her tripping on the fruit
Spilling from the gigantic wicker cornucopia,
Her besmattered.

If dignity is an island
Surrounded by sharks, or a silo
Way below ground with titanium doors,
Or two spies sent to this planet
In perfect drag,

Then it might be okay to teeter somewhere
Between blank and overfull,
But since it isn't and doesn't and really
Is about as mysterious as the satisfaction
Of a son razzing his mom at a pizza place,

Cathy balked. Ah, the party, the hats
So much about making friends
As if they were crafts and shaping
Their envy into joy, so much about sugar.
And after, in the basement, alone:

Little Cathy, half a Dixie cup of tang,
Stood before the clown painted on the wall
With its red yarn pompom nose,
Before the gold plaster of paris King Tut
Death mask and the malformed and malcolored
But gigantic tulips, and wept.

There
At the bottom of the basement steps
None of this felt like anything,
Only the donkey poster, or the place
Where a donkey was before
Each eyehole, orifice,

Each inch of hide
Got pinned with tails, got argus-assed,
Got sadder than any fall from the heights
Of two cupsworth sugar and two impeccable
But useless tantrums.

i.

Her discovery
of her own self-evidence
made her a star.

Jojo didn't rely
on denied decay or the allure
of flaunted failure.

Instead, she gave in.
She'd never liked
being young

so to age, ravaged
as she was, tickled
that in us

that also wants
to give
in

without
having to make
allowances for others.

Jojo had funhouse
mirrors throughout
her house,

and a full
working carousel
that when set to high

would splash
across the courtyard's
stainless steel tiles

and claw
up glass walls
and over end tables,

that forced
thoughts of old books
and their oil-emulsion end papers

or just made you barf.
But Jojo loved this proof
that wanting backwards

is wavy
like a movie flashback
brewing

but never taking.

Superheroes were the worst.
They were either too re-
or too unrealistic.

The set a blue screen
and a floorfull
of reflective tape.

The latex outfit
didn't breathe despite
the "mummy cover"

as they called it.
All red with
rat ears

Jojo felt
simply
taken advantage of,

though she'd gross
on this one
while the arty film

about dolphins
would languish profitless.
Clowns had

replaced them this season
for favourite fish.
Red as coals

she'd been in
a terrible
foundry accident

part of FDR's WPA
and come out smoldering
and Republican.

Her power was transforming
objects to meanings
and sometimes

meanings to people,
but they were always
malformed,

well, frankly,
grotesque,
and never really got

the or any point across
except –
and Jojo

understood this as
Vat Woman's greatest message –
language fails

so why not
best it
by failing

it?
Impeccable
as this superheroine's

logic was,
fans took
a different message

entirely –
that washed up,
plain,

nay, downright ugly,
actresses
could get famous

for being famous
and wash their red-
clad swaths

over acres of snow white
where never
however much you'd hope

or they'd pay or pray,
however much an entire
industry

mustered its collective
capital could they
not even in epics

or in the most tear-stained
women's films
nor in realist political dramas
.

in none of them
across no span
of the visual field

would Jojo
or her like
leave footprints.

k.

Barb's egg salad had the jags
squares and domes
common final thoughts of mormons.

And it seemed a shame
she chose –
what with the devoted

and treasured
cut-glass dishes –
not to devil them.

Of course, no one
noticed really,
blindfolded as they were

in protest
against lookism.
They'd decided

that sitting still
was not
fighting back enough

so to be truly
political
they took a handicap.

Mary Ellen drank
undiet soda
unknowingly

and was filled
with an absence
she'd only last

felt at her mother's funeral
when she banged the rose
having tripped

on the fake grass
carpet round the grave,
down on the coffin

and nailed her siblings'
thorns, already placed,
into her forearm.

It was while
in a side room
plain as a high school

an assistant
smelling of surgery
cleaned and wrapped

her wrist
and looked
into her eyes

for thanks. She had none
and hated herself
for it. She avoided

the grave, didn't dispute
the extortionate bill,
wouldn't let herself

look full upon the wound
until, bandages entirely
unnecessary,

and iodine
beside the point,
she saw

when she connected
the scabs:
The Big Dipper.

Jojo had
a wonderful time
here among the girls

but you'd never
tell
since Cathy

told her
that all American culture
was calculated to

fuck women over,
so when they said,
"don't frown

you'll get frown lines," you knew
it was precisely
not frowning

that brought them on.
So below her
luscious silk blindfold

Jojo frowned, forming
a near perfect
parabola

with little arrows
at each end
of her expression's asymptotic reach.

And Tootles
whose eyes
were her best feature

hoped
this revolution
bloody

and failed.
It seemed
her sacrifice

was twice
the others'.
And right she was –

when Marge
cast off her sash
in interest

of distinguishing jams.
Detesting gooseberries
because they cannot be pronounced.

Her shocked gasp
broke the spell.
There was

no jam whatever
to choose from.
Also shocked,

in a halo round
Peg's head
a hundred hornets

descended
while all looked on
helplessly

proving their point
quite elegantly
really

while Peg
had pressed upon her dark curls
a yellow shimmering crown.

1.

She was sure
that the lack
of anyone

she truly loved
was all
kept

God
from asking
sacrifice.

Mostly his requests
involved cleaning.
And this

made religion
seem part
of the growing

service economy.
She nearly took
to church

but understood
that the way painters do
what's done by numbers.

The ages made sense
with their solitaries
and celibates –

what baffled Rita
was the just plain
dearth

of good nature.
All eyes on plates
or rotty corpses

at roll call.
Oh, Rita mused,
why not knit?

Since she was given the fire,
the exact address
of the everyday miraculous,

why not ring,
and be had in
for tea?

m.

Stiff as characters
in first novels
in they filed.

Sat. This one
a snot eater.
That one a thief.

When the fireball
blazed of a sudden
dead center

none were surprised.
Myth was they figured
always after all

something wrong
and here
maybe it too

felt the call
to introduce itself
on that

seductively routine
firstname basis
and beam

around the circle
at the turnout.

And it understood
the creed: no one
ever

got better.
It loved a spring-fed
pond in Vermont

where
plummeting to earth
it first glimpsed

its fall.
The algae brilliantined.
The willows

puffs of fireworks,
the fish drawn up
to gape.

None of the group
really understood
though, each

her own
matchstick poised
on a water glass.

But they nodded.
And in the language
of fire

that meant precisely
what this ball
knew but couldn't be.

How had *they*,
it puzzled,
with their delicious

redemptions
and woe,
so perfectly posed

and then answered
the riddle
of desire.

As if their therapeutic
language
took them

in its dry palms
and guided
the nods.

The up.
And the down
of it. The blank

blanket of yes
over steaming meat piles
of no.

At that moment a loud laugh shattered the air and,
looking up, he saw a large parrot sitting on a tree,
cleaning the few feathers he had left.

"Why are you laughing?" asked Pinocchio angrily.

"I am laughing because while cleaning my feathers,
I tickled myself under my wings."

The puppet did not answer. He went to the dam,
filled his old shoe with water again,

and watered the earth covering his money.

Carlo Collodi

ACKNOWLEDGMENTS

"a," "b," "c," "d," "e," "f," "g," "h," and "i" appeared in *Slope*.

"V" and "IX" first appeared in *Sonora Review*.

"VI," "XI," "XII," "j," and "k" appeared in *Spork*.